and the Ecclesiastical Monuments of Wigtown District

C A Ralegh Radford, MA, D LITT, FSA, FR HIST S, FBA
and **Gordon Donaldson,** CBE, MA, PhD, D LITT, FR HIST S

with revisions and additions by **Ian Fisher,** MA, FSA, FSA Scot
and **Christopher J Tabraham,** BA, FSA Scot

Historic Buildings and Monuments
Scottish Development Department

Edinburgh
Her Majesty's Stationery Office

MONUMENTS TO CHRISTIANITY

Whithorn, the scene of the earliest recorded Christian mission to Scotland, became an important Celtic monastery. It was later converted into a house of Premonstratensian canons and the great church served as the cathedral of the medieval bishops of Galloway. Both church and monastery were suppressed in the sixteenth century. Later, the nave was adapted as the cathedral of the Protestant bishops. In the eighteenth century it was used as the Presbyterian parish church. The present church was built in 1822 and the older structure then became a ruin. The site of the destroyed buildings was, until recently, used as a cemetery.

In 1908 the HM Office of Works were constituted guardians of the buildings, which had recently been partly cleared and restored by the Marquess of Bute. A small building at the gate to the churchyard was at the same time formed into a museum to house the crosses and inscriptions found in and around Whithorn.

The Secretary of State for Scotland is also guardian of St Ninian's Chapel at the Isle of Whithorn; St Ninian's Cave, Glasserton; Chapel Finian, north of Port William; Laggangairn standing stones, north of Glenluce; and of the early memorial stones found at Kirkmadrine, an ancient church site in the Rhinns of Galloway.

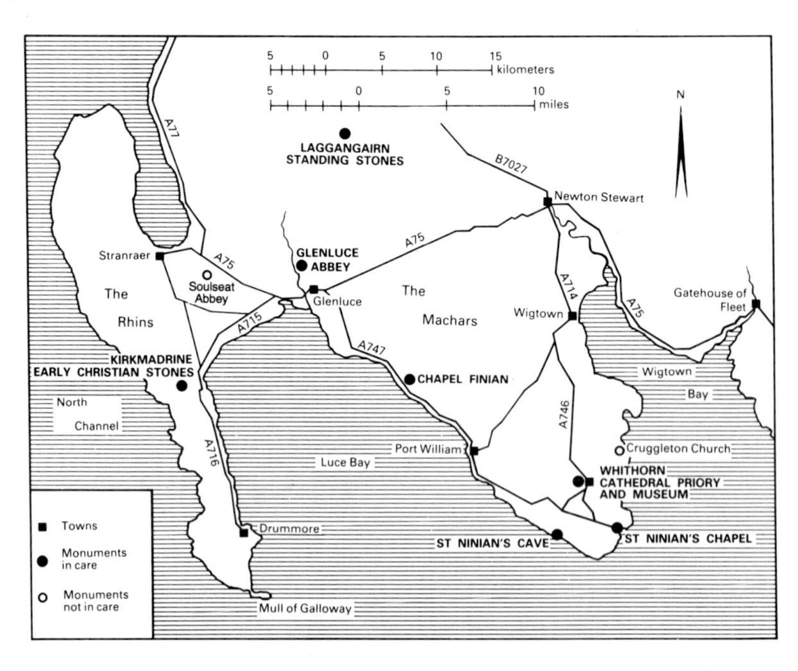

THE EARLIEST CHRISTIAN MISSION

St Ninian and the Beginnings of Christianity in Scotland

Christianity reached southern Britain whilst it was still a province of the Roman empire. We cannot tell how soon the new faith had penetrated beyond the frontiers of the empire. At the beginning of the third century Tertullian wrote of regions in Britain, inaccessible to Rome, yet subject to Christ. We cannot dismiss this and other statements by Christian authors as empty rhetoric but must assume that there was a slow penetration by individual Christians into the remoter parts of these islands.

With the fifth century came a more determined effort to convert the whole Celtic world. St Ninian in southern Scotland belonged to this new missionary effort, which within a century effected the conversion of those regions lying on and beyond the old frontier of the empire. Of St Ninian we know little. Bede, our oldest authority, wrote 300 years later. He records the tradition that the southern Picts, renouncing idolatry, had accepted the true faith at the preaching of Ninian, 'a most reverend and holy man of the British race'. He adds that Ninian had been taught at Rome and that he was buried with many other saints in his cathedral church which was named after St Martin of Tours. Finally, he gives the information that this cathedral was commonly known as the 'White House' (*Candida Casa*) since it possessed a church of stone, a thing unusual among the Britons. The mention of St Martin shows that the building of this church took place after his death in 397. Bede incidentally refers the mission of St Ninian to a period long before the arrival of St Columba at Iona, which took place in 563. The naming of the church at Whithorn after the famous bishop of Tours may indicate that St Ninian had studied in the school established in that city which is known to have been frequented by Britons and others seeking learning.

The Celtic Monastery of Whithorn

A great monastery, such as arose at Whithorn, was a community of missionaries, scholars and other

Reliquary of St Ninian: this is thought to have come from the priory and dates from around 1200 AD. The reliquary held fragments of the True Cross. The collar bears an inscription to various saints headed by the Saints Ninian and Andrew. (Reproduced by kind permission of the British Museum)

An aerial view of Whithorn and its priory.

individuals, each serving God in his own way. The organisation belonged to one of the oldest Christian traditions, originating in Egypt and the East and reaching Britain by way of Gaul.

The monastery would have comprised a group of small, scattered buildings enclosed within a fence or high bank. The buildings were simple structures, perhaps of dry-stone construction, possibly of wood. There may have been several churches, a library and scriptorium, in which manuscripts were copied. There would have been a guest-house and dwellings for the monks. Barns and store-houses were also required for the produce of the land tilled by the monks and for food rents from estates given to the community. All these were placed without set plan, individual buildings being grouped together as convenience might dictate. Among them stood great crosses of wood or stone commemorating important events in the history of the monastery or the life of its founder. Beside the principal church, in which the founder would have lain enshrined, was the cemetery. Burial there was not confined to members of the community but was a privilege sought by all, under the impression that interment near the patron would best ensure their welfare in the hereafter.

The heart of the monastery lay on the small rounded hill west of the main street on which the ruins of the medieval cathedral now stand. The full extent of the monastery is unknown. Many early monasteries covered a considerable area and this may be true of St Ninian's foundation also. The stone of St Peter (No. 2, p. 27) used to stand 800 m away beside the road to the Isle of Whithorn and may have marked the site of an area named in honour of the Apostle. If the stone was in its original position it would indicate that the monastic settlement extended at least so far.

The arrangement of the monastery founded by St Martin at Tours inspired many Celtic foundations. We know from

"St Peter" Stone (No. 2). The inscription reads: (L) OCI/ PETRI APU/ STOLI "The place of Peter the Apostle"

contemporary accounts that the establishment there included not only the monastery proper but a retreat outside the city on the bank of the Loire. To that retreat the bishop himself and his followers went from time to time to live a life of contemplation. There are literary references to these retreats and at Whithorn we have a probable example—the cave at Physgill, 5 km away. This does not figure in the written sources but the series of votive crosses, both cut on the wall and incised on stones, marks it out as a place connected with St Ninian.

There is a third site in the neighbourhood traditionally associated with St Ninian—the chapel at the Isle of Whithorn. The present building is a ruin dating from the thirteenth century, probably erected for the convenience of pilgrims and other travellers coming to Whithorn by sea. It may conceivably have marked the site where St Ninian himself landed and from which his mission started, but no older remains have yet been positively identified and no early Christian crosses or other relics have been recovered from the Isle.

The Northumbrian Supremacy at Whithorn

The monastery founded by St Ninian became a famous seat of learning, known throughout the Celtic world. Scholars from Ireland resorted there in the fifth and sixth centuries and monks from Whithorn acted as missionaries to other parts of Scotland. But British rule was threatened by the advance of Anglian Northumbria.

The Northumbrians set up a bishopric in the old Celtic monastery at Whithorn. Pechthelm, the first bishop, was consecrated shortly before 731. He was a friend of Bede, the historian, who probably obtained some of his information about St Ninian from this source. Bede himself and the old Northumbrian annals have preserved the names of the bishops who succeeded Pechthelm during the eighth century. After 802 our sources fail but there is no reason to think that the See did not

St Ninian's Cave. Tradition has long associated this cave with St Ninian.

continue as long as Northumbria held sway in Galloway.

Few remains of this period have survived at Whithorn. The Anglian monastery, if we may judge from the excavated remains at Whitby, would have differed little from its Celtic predecessor. But none of the buildings has been found. Two crosses from Whithorn itself (Nos. 3 and 5, p. 28) have ornament characteristic of the ninth century. St Ninian continued to be the patron of Whithorn. He lay enshrined in the church and towards the end of the eighth century the famous scholar, Alcuin, sent a gift of silken garments in which to wrap the body.

Our last picture of the Northumbrian community at Whithorn belongs to the end of the ninth century. Halfdan, the Danish king, had conquered the Northumbrian capital, York, and settled his followers in the surrounding countryside. Disaster overtook the whole land and the monks of Lindisfarne, bearing the relics of their patron, St Cuthbert, left the island, seeking a safer refuge. After many journeyings they tried to cross to Ireland but were driven back by a storm and found temporary refuge at Whithorn where the Northumbrian monastery was still in existence. It was at Whithorn that they found cast up on the beach the precious Lindisfarne Gospels which had fallen from the boat.

The Viking Age in Galloway

The Vikings from Scandinavia, who had first raided the coasts of Britain in search of plunder, soon began to settle in these islands. We have no record of the conquest of Galloway, but the scanty evidence suggests that it took place about 920. The evidence of the place-names and of the crosses shows that the Norsemen were established most closely in the Machars.

Whithorn being at the centre of Norse settlement, here, beside the old shrine of St

Ninian, the new ruling class buried their dead. The site has produced parts of some twenty standing crosses dating from this period, small headstones designed to mark individual graves. Similar memorials have been found at St Ninian's Cave and elsewhere. The only structure that can be associated with this age is the simple rectangular church at Chapel Finian, in the parish of Mochrum.

Ecclesiastical Reform in the Twelfth Century and the Foundation of the Premonstratensian Priory

In France the tenth century saw the foundation of the Abbey of Cluny, the mother-house of a reformed Benedictine order of monks, which aimed at re-establishing the early vigour and discipline of monastic rule. During the following two centuries the movement of reform spread across the whole of Western Europe. Galloway was no exception.

Norse rule must have come to an end soon after 1100 and some twenty years later Earl David, who ruled the southern part of the kingdom during the lifetime of his elder brother, Alexander I, was receiving dues from Galloway. The province was then, or shortly after, under the rule of Fergus, a member of King David's court.

The first reform carried out under Fergus was the re-establishment at Whithorn of the bishopric which seems to have lapsed during the period of Norse rule. Gilla-Aldan, by his name also a native of Galloway, was the first of the new line of bishops. He was consecrated by Archbishop Thurstan of York in, or soon after, 1128 and the Romanesque cathedral was erected shortly after.

The arrival of the reformed monastic orders in Galloway marks a further stage of ecclesiastical reorganisation. The earliest of these houses may have been Soulseat on the Green Loch where, in 1147, the great Irish reformer, St Malachi, is said to have established a Cistercian abbey. If this was indeed the case, it seems not to have flourished and Bishop Christian, who was consecrated to the See of Galloway in 1154, was an advocate of the Premonstratensians. Soulseat was transferred to this Order and was colonised from Prémontré itself. Whithorn became a daughter-house of Soulseat about 1177, though there is evidence to suggest that it too had been established a little earlier, colonised perhaps by Augustinian canons.

The Premonstratensian Priory

The Premonstratensians, called White Canons from the colour of their habit, were canons regular—that is, like the better known Augustinians, or Black Canons, their work was not confined to the monastery. From it they went out to preach and conduct services in parish churches. Within the monastery, the Premonstratensians followed the Cistercian example of stressing the need for manual labour as well as strict religious observance.

The first prior, presumably before it became a Premonstratensian house, was Adam or Edan. 'William, prior of Galloway' is referred to in the 1160's and a prior called Michael is described as the first prior of the Premonstratensian priory, that is, from about 1177. Very little is known about the history of the priory for a long period after its foundation, as no register of the house has survived. We do not even have the names of all the priors and those which we have are known simply through a bare mention of them in a charter or similar source.

The Priory as Cathedral

The priory church was the cathedral of the diocese of Galloway. The bishops, although popularly known as 'bishops of Galloway' were nearly always officially styled 'of Whithorn'. In almost all the Scottish bishoprics the cathedral was served by secular canons, that is, priests who were not members of any religious order, but the

The priory nave from the north. The featureless side wall of the nave separated the church from the cloister.

Premonstratensian canons of Whithorn formed a cathedral chapter of regulars. It was because the canons' church was the cathedral of the diocese that its head was called a prior and not an abbot, since the bishop stood in place of the abbot. There must have been a house for the bishop at Whithorn and in 1408, when the twelve canons were ordered to pay half of their revenues for ten years to help repair the cathedral, they were also commanded to build up the episcopal residence. There would presumably also be accommodation for the consistorial court of the diocese, which had a wide jurisdiction, particularly in matrimonial and testamentary matters. The canons, as the chapter, had to give their consent to certain acts of the bishops, especially in the disposal of land and other property belonging to the bishopric. In short, the priory was the administrative centre of the diocese.

The canons, as the cathedral chapter, also obtained the right of electing the bishop although their part in the proceedings was often merely formal, the effective voice lying elsewhere. The bishopric had existed before the priory was established and even after its foundation the canons did not at once become the electoral body. The earlier mode of election had been nominally by 'the clergy and people' of the diocese, a formula which possibly concealed the effective voice of the lords of Galloway who claimed the 'patronage' of their bishopric. It may be assumed that the earliest bishops were chosen in this way. The chapter first attempted to assert a right to election in 1235 following the death of Bishop Walter, but their candidate, one of their own number called Odo, was rejected in favour of Gilbert, abbot of Glenluce, who had been elected 'by the clergy and people' and who enjoyed the favour of the king. Twenty years later there was another dispute. Henry, abbot of Holyrood, seems at first to have been elected by the clergy and people with the support of the king. Opposition came from John Balliol, who had married Lady Dervorgilla, heiress of Galloway, and considered that he had the right of patronage. Bishop Henry, however, maintained his position and strengthened it by a fresh election, this time by the canons of Whithorn. After this dispute had ended with a recognition of the canons' right, nothing more is heard of the claims of clergy and people. Yet an election might still be the occasion of dissension between powerful laymen who wished to nominate the bishop. In 1294, when the chapter chose Thomas de Kirkcudbright, the chaplain of Robert Bruce, Lord of Annandale, the election was opposed, unsuccessfully, by the younger John Balliol, son of Lady Dervorgilla and now King of Scots.

Experience had shown that local electors were liable to pressure from a secular power—either the king or a local magnate—and this was one of the motives which prompted or encouraged the popes to take episcopal appointments into their own hands. Simon, abbot of Holyrood, bishop of Whithorn from 1327 until after 1354, and his successor, Michael Makenlagh (1355–59), who had been prior of Whithorn, were elected by the chapter, but thereafter, right down to the Reformation, the pope exercised the right to 'provide' the bishops. The chapter, with irrepressible optimism, continued from time to time to hold elections but if its choice conflicted with that of the pope its decision was set aside. Although appointments were being made by the pope it was often men with a local connection who were chosen. Ninian Spot (1458–82), canon of Dunkeld and Comptroller of Scotland, was an exception.

In earlier times the bishopric of Galloway was reckoned one of the poorest in Scotland. From 1504, however, the bishops of Galloway were also deans of the Chapel Royal of Stirling and from 1531 they enjoyed the revenues of the abbey of Tongland. These annexations made the bishopric more valuable and at the period of the Reformation its annual income was some £1,200 in money with quantities of barley, meal, malt and salmon worth perhaps £300 or more.

This crozier, dated to the late twelfth century, was found in one of two graves excavated at the priory. The human figures on the crozier are representations of prophets, each holding a book or scroll, and, in the lowest part, four bishops. The crozier probably belonged to a bishop of the see of Whithorn. (Reproduced by kind permission of the Royal Museum of Scotland)

Whithorn's Connection with York

As the Scottish Church had no archbishop until 1472 the archbishops of York had an opportunity to claim the primacy of Scotland. In the twelfth century they strove hard to secure the subjection to them of all the Scottish bishoprics. After a prolonged dispute the pope, in 1192, declared that the Scottish Church was subject only to Rome and to no archbishops, but Galloway was not included among the Scottish sees which were thus freed from English supremacy. Down to at least 1355 each successive bishop of Whithorn formally gave obedience to the archbishop of York. Not only this, but most of them also acted as part-time assistants to the archbishops, frequently performing episcopal functions south of the Border; it seems very likely that they were prompted to do so by the need to supplement the scanty revenues of their own bishopric.

Until the Wars of Independence the relationship of Whithorn with York raised no difficulties. Like so many of the great nobles of the time, including the Balliols and the Bruces, the bishops were simply Anglo-Scots, equally at home on both sides of the Border. With Edward I's conquest of Scotland and the subsequent war of liberation, however, such divided allegiance became an embarrassment. Thomas de Kirkcudbright, who had become bishop of Galloway in 1294, seems to have been a client of the Bruce family and he attached himself to the patriotic cause under Robert Bruce, who became king in 1306. The pope was supporting the English cause and King Robert had incurred excommunication for murdering the Red Comyn in the church at Dumfries, but Bishop Thomas was one of the Scottish churchmen who defied both the pope and the English monarch by formally declaring for Robert I in 1310. When the war was over and Scotland's independence recognised Whithorn received the liberator king as a pilgrim in 1329. He came but three months before his death, an invalid making a last desperate effort to find a remedy for the leprosy of which he died.

Thomas de Kirkcudbright was the last bishop to act as a suffragan in England; his successor, Simon, attempted without success to establish the same direct relationship with the pope which the other Scottish bishops enjoyed, and Bishop Michael (1355-59) was the last bishop whose profession of obedience to the English archbishop is recorded. Yet the connection survived, albeit tenuously, until the period of the Great Schism. From 1378 England recognised the pope at Rome, Scotland an anti-pope at Avignon, and there were for a time two rival bishops of Galloway, Oswald recognised by York and acknowledging the pope but unable, except at the risk of his life, to set foot in his diocese, and Thomas de Rossy, acknowledging the anti-pope and accepted by the Scots. The Scottish candidate wrote a treatise in support of the anti-pope and had such strong views on his cause that he concluded by challenging any English bishop to meet him in personal combat to decide the issue.

After Bishop Thomas' vigorous challenge to the English bishops and their pope nothing more is heard of obedience to York, even after the schism was healed in 1418. In 1430 the Scottish king declared that Galloway was on the same footing as the other Scottish bishoprics. Papal recognition of the severance from York came in 1472, when the see of St Andrews was erected into an archbishopric and Galloway made one of its suffragans. Twenty years later, when Glasgow was raised to archi-episcopal status, Galloway was transferred to its jurisdiction.

Whithorn as a Place of Pilgrimage

The shrine of St Ninian at Whithorn was for centuries one of the most famous of Scotland's places of pilgrimage, attracting visitors from all parts of the British Isles

Looking through the barrel-vaulted crypt. Here lay the relics of St Ninian, visited by many pilgrims throughout the medieval period.

and overseas. In 1302, when Prince Edward, afterwards Edward II of England, was in command of one of his father's armies of occupation, it became known that he was coming to the shrine as a pilgrim and it is said that the Scots attempted to disappoint him by removing the saint's image to Sweetheart Abbey from which it was miraculously transported back to Whithorn. Robert the Bruce's pilgrimage has already been mentioned. His son, David II, also visited Whithorn. During his defeat by the English at Neville's Cross in 1346, two arrow-heads had lodged in his body and we are told that one of them resisted every attempt at extraction until he came to the shrine. In 1427 James I issued a safe-conduct to persons coming to Whithorn on pilgrimage from England and the Isle of Man. They were to come either by sea (from Man) or by way of the West March (from England) and to return by the same routes, to bear themselves as pilgrims and to remain in Scotland no more than fifteen days; they were to wear openly on their habits one badge as they came and another (to be received from the prior of Whithorn) on their return journey. Several references suggest that the traffic of pilgrims to and from Whithorn was a conspicuous feature on the roads and through the towns and villages of Galloway in the fifteenth century. In 1441 when Margaret, Countess of Douglas, petitioned the pope for an indulgence for the rebuilding of a bridge over the River Bladnoch, one reason given was that it was at a place 'where pilgrims to St Ninian assemble'. James III, IV and V all went on pilgrimage to Whithorn.

Gifts must have come to the shrine from many quarters. In 1434, when a Frenchman and his Scots companion were on their way to Scotland, they had a narrow escape from disaster through a storm at sea and in their peril swore that they would make an offering to St Ninian; when at last they landed safely they went to Whithorn and presented a silver model of a ship, engraved with the arms of the king of France. The treasures of Whithorn have long been dispersed. It is said that an arm of St Ninian was saved from his shrine at the Reformation and passed through the hands of Alexander McWhirrie, a notorious Scottish Jesuit, into the keeping of the Scots seminary at Douai where it probably remained until the French Revolution.

The Lands and Churches of the Priory

The priory drew its revenues largely from the rents (and, later, the feu-duties) of its landed estates. Little is known of the endowments which it possessed before the War of Independence but immediately after there were charters by Edward Bruce, Lord of Galloway, and Thomas Randolph, Lord of Annandale and Man, and a confirmation by Robert Bruce. Other gifts followed and the estates ultimately belonging to the priory lay not only in the neighbourhood of Whithorn but in many parts of Galloway and in Carrick. There were outlying possessions in Kintyre and the Isle of Man. The prior of Whithorn, along with two local lairds, supplied thirty-six oxen to draw one of the guns which were taken by the Scots to Flodden. Apart from land, revenues came from the teinds, or tithes, of the parish churches annexed to the priory—nearly twenty in all, mostly in Galloway. By the Reformation the total annual revenues were worth in the order of £3,000.

The burgh of Whithorn, which had received charters from Robert I and David II, was granted to the prior and convent by James II in 1451. The priors fostered the trade of the burgh and of the Isle of Whithorn, which chiefly comprised the purchase of skins, wool, hides and cloth in the hinterland for exporting in return for wine, wax and corn. The priory owned ships engaged in this commerce. The prior was entitled to the customs on goods passing through Whithorn but it seems that for some time before the Reformation he had difficulty in collecting them and between 1553–57 we find him pursuing Alexander Stewart of Garlies for appropriating the great customs of the Isle of Whithorn for the whole period since 1526.

The Reformation

Henry Macdowell, who seems to have died in 1514, was probably the last genuine prior. Thereafter, in common with most religious houses, Whithorn was held by commendators who enjoyed the fruits but did not perform the duties of the office. Immediately after Macdowell's death there was a disputed succession, arising from the strained relations between Scotland and Rome.

In 1515, the Duke of Albany, governor of Scotland on behalf of the infant James V, nominated Alexander Stewart, his half-brother, to the position but the pope nominated an Italian cardinal and never gave Alexander confirmation. In 1518, when it became possible to reach an amicable agreement with Rome, the Italian claimant renounced his title in favour of Gavin Dunbar, who became commendator. Dunbar was tutor to James V and held the priory until he became archbishop of Glasgow in 1524.

After Gavin Dunbar's departure the priory came into the hands of the Fleming family. Whithorn now was little more than a secular lordship, hereditary in a noble family. Meantime the number of monks was in decline, falling to around sixteen by the Reformation. By this time the ideals of the order were being lost sight of by the canons as well as by the commendators, for, while the commendator was chiefly concerned with his rents, the canons were enjoying their share of the revenues and the fewer they were in number the larger the portion there was for each. They became comfortable pensioners, each living in his private quarters. With diminishing zeal and the diversion of funds to private ends the buildings were inevitably neglected.

At the Reformation Galloway had a bishop who joined the reformers, Alexander Gordon, a brother of the Earl of Huntly. He took up the cause of reform in his diocese and persuaded a great many of his clergy to join in the work of the reformed church. Out of eleven monks at Whithorn known to be alive in 1560 no less than seven acted as ministers or readers under the new regime, in Whithorn and neighbouring parishes. All the canons, whether or not they acted in this way, still enjoyed their portions or pensions in lieu thereof at the rate of £26 13s. 4d. annually and there are references to their continued occupation of their 'chambers' or quarters at the priory. The last of the canons died shortly after 1590. Meanwhile, the prior of Whithorn, Malcolm Fleming, unlike the

A silver chalice and paten, dated to the thirteenth century, found in one of the graves excavated at the priory. The chalice is an undecorated silver bowl. The paten is of silver-gilt, in the centre of which is an engraving of the "Manus Dei" (Hand of God) making the sign of the blessing. (Reproduced by kind permission of the Royal Museum of Scotland)

bishop and the majority of the clergy, did not welcome the Reformation and was actually prosecuted for using the Latin service after it had been forbidden by parliament.

When Malcolm Fleming died in 1569, the priory was gifted to Lord Robert Stewart, an illegitimate son of James V and half-brother of Queen Mary. The Flemings, however, considered the benefice at their private disposal and for some years maintained a rival candidate against whom Lord Robert had difficulty in securing effective possession. On his death in 1581, the Crown gifted the priory to Patrick Stewart, the son of another of James V's sons—Robert Stewart, Earl of Orkney—nephew of the preceding commendator. Patrick, like his father, was notorious as a tyrannical ruler of the Northern Isles. When his estates were for a time forfeited the priory was, in 1605, united to the bishopric of Galloway to help provide an adequate income for the bishops of the reformed church.

Later History

Though the priory can be held to have ceased to exist with the demise of the last canon shortly after 1590, the bishopric continued intermittently for another century. After Bishop George Gordon's death in 1588 there was a vacancy of seventeen years, the church being for a time under presbyterian government. In 1605 Gavin Hamilton was appointed bishop who, like other bishops, recovered the bishopric lands from the Crown in 1606 and was subsequently restored to full episcopal powers.

Watercolour of Whithorn, painted by I Clark shortly after the erection of the new parish church in 1822.

The episcopal succession was again interrupted during a second presbyterian interlude, between 1638 and 1661, and in 1690 presbyterian government was finally established in the Church of Scotland. The last of the bishops of Galloway of the Scottish establishment, deprived in 1689, died in 1726 having outlived all his colleagues.

Though there were bishops in the Church between the Reformation and the Revolution of 1689 the cathedral at Whithorn was never as important an ecclesiastical centre after the Reformation as it had been earlier. It is true that a chapter of ministers in the diocese was set up to take over the functions of the canons in formally electing bishops and in signifying their assent to the bishops' charter by appending their signatures and attaching the chapter seal, but while these acts sometimes took place at Whithorn, they did not necessarily do so and there were no resident canons conducting cathedral services as there were in England. When meetings of the diocesan synod are recorded, between 1664 and 1671, they took place chiefly at Wigtown, never at Whithorn, and it was at Wigtown in about 1588 that the presbytery was established.

For a time, in the late sixteenth and early seventeenth centuries, the church was actually roofless and disused but the nave was reconstructed, probably by Bishop Gavin Hamilton (consecrated 1610). It served as a cathedral as long as there were bishops and then, after 1689, as the parish church until 1822 when the present one was built nearby. The west tower, which was still standing in 1684, fell early in the following century thereby necessitating the rebuilding of the west gable. There was, of course, no need to maintain the priory buildings generally but it may be that a part of them was in use for a time as school or school-house. In 1633, at a time when the bishops were given fresh powers to establish schools, we find Bishop Lamb disponing to George Gladstanes, schoolmaster and reader at Whithorn, 'all and haill the yairdis within the precincts and closage of the abbacie'. As the buildings fell into decay the site was utilised as a burying place for the burgh and parish.

CHURCH, CAVE AND CROSS

Whithorn Cathedral-Priory

The cathedral-priory lies on a small hill west of the main street of the burgh. The approach is by a narrow lane known as The Pend which passes under the arch of the old gatehouse to the priory. This building dates from around 1500, with later features.

The Priory Church

The visible remains of the church now consist of two separate parts—the nave to the west and the crypt and other structures to the east, which were largely reconstructed at the end of the nineteenth century—the central section of the church is now covered by the burial ground. The earliest walls seen protruding from the east end of the medieval church were part of the early Christian church. Above this was built the twelfth-century cathedral, which was subsequently incorporated in the

The nave of the cathedral-priory from the east. The complex architecture of the walls highlights the frequent changes in church organisation from the twelfth to the nineteenth centuries.

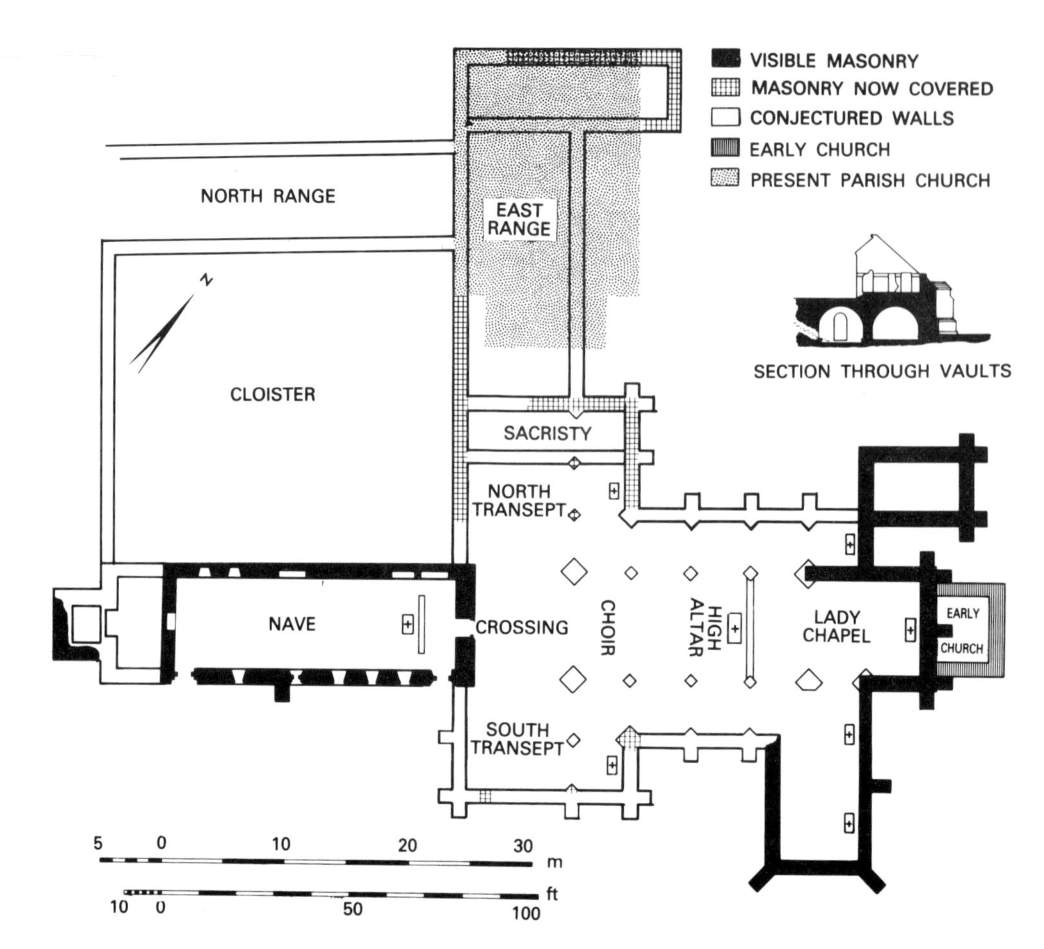

Plan of Whithorn cathedral-priory.

Plan of the nave.

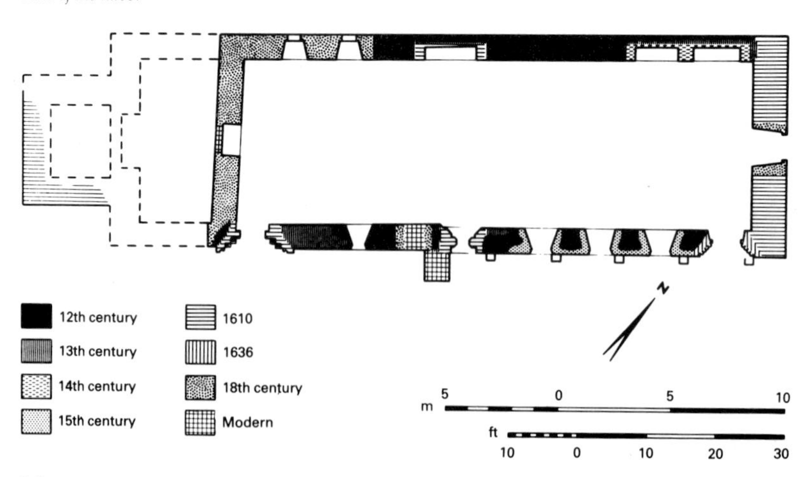

The Romanesque doorway: this elaborate doorway is not in its original position. Part of it may have come from the crossing of the twelfth-century cathedral or from one of the eastern chapels.

thirteenth-century priory church. The full extent of the first medieval cathedral is not known. Part of the intervening space between the nave and the crypt has been excavated and the results would suggest that the priory church possessed both north and south transepts, with an aisled choir and an eastern chapel behind the high altar. Of the cloister and conventual buildings to the north little now survives.

The Nave

The nave is basically of two periods. The eastern part still has twelfth-century masonry at the base of the side walls with the western part representing a thirteenth-century extension which effectively doubled its length. The present main entrance is through the Romanesque doorway at the west end of the south wall. It is now disfigured by the slot cut for the gable roof of a porch; the recesses for benches can be seen near the ground.

The west wall and the western part of the north wall belong to the early eighteenth-century rebuilding when the nave was shortened following the collapse of the west tower, which itself had only been built early in the seventeenth century. A wide gallery sloping downwards extended across the end of the church. The stone corbels carrying the floor of this gallery can be seen built into the north wall and inserted into the medieval south wall. A tall narrow window penetrates the west gable, so lighting the gallery. The lower part was later converted into a doorway, to which an external stair led up. There is a small rectangular window in the base of this wall, below the gallery, and others of the same type in the side wall, lighting both the gallery and the space beneath. A lofty lancet window with sandstone dressings is the only original feature in the western half of the nave.

The eastern part of the side walls is medieval, mostly of the thirteenth century. No twelfth-century masonry is visible inside the church but the base of the ashlar face-work and buttressing of this date can be seen outside the south wall. Three large windows, originally of two lights of tracery, were inserted in this wall early in the fifteenth century. These windows then reached to the top of the wall. They were cut down when the wall was lowered and the rougher arched heads now existing are of the early seventeenth century. Further west the central part of this wall has been rebuilt. The elaborately moulded window is of sixteenth-century type and as its head corresponds to the height of the post-Reformation roof level it must be considered part of the rebuilding.

At the east end of this south wall is a second inserted doorway. The inner arch is of the thirteenth century but the outer arch is richly moulded work of about 1500. The finials of the hood mould are carved with angels bearing a shield on which are the arms of Bishop George Vaus (1492–1508). The door was inserted to provide access to the east end of the Protestant cathedral when a liturgical east end and fixed altar were introduced by Bishop Sydserf (1635–38).

The old part of the north wall is now windowless. In the medieval period the cloister lay on this side and corbels carrying the pentice, or sloping, roof of the south (nearest) cloister walk can be seen outside. Above this roof was a range of small lancet windows. These were destroyed when the wall was cut down but the sills of two remain in position.

The east wall is of post-Reformation date. It is built on the base of the *pulpitum*, or stone screen, which can be seen projecting from the outer face. The great east window, with its pointed head and chamfered jambs, is an original feature designed for the Protestant cathedral. The lower part of the opening was later filled with a rectangular wooden frame to accommodate which part of the jambs was cut away. The door below is an eighteenth-century insertion.

The only medieval fittings remaining in the nave are three tomb recesses. The oldest, of the twelfth century, was largely destroyed when the door at the east end of the south wall was inserted. Only one stone now remains, below the present ground level. The other two, which have cusped arches and richly decorated detail, have been inserted at the east end of the north wall. They date from about 1300 and stand on the level of the medieval floor. The western arch has been damaged and

The interior of the nave looking towards the west end. Many of the architectural features were introduced after the Reformation.

the missing parts made good with fragments of fifteenth-century sculpture. There is a fourth tomb recess in the centre of the north wall. It has a plain round-headed arch dating from the early seventeenth century and was probably inserted for the burial of one of the Protestant bishops of Galloway.

The East End

The thirteenth-century Premonstratensian church extended further east than the twelfth-century cathedral, leaving space for a crypt beneath. The walls of this crypt were restored by the Marquess of Bute at the end of the nineteenth century as high as the floor level of the medieval church and are finished as a low parapet enclosing a paved area representing the east end. The restoration included the southern chapel of about 1500.

The length of the eastern arm of the thirteenth-century church (28 m) is too great for the whole to have formed the monastic choir and presbytery, for the choir is known to have extended westward into the central crossing. It is therefore clear that the high altar stood against a screen wall extending from pier to pier four bays east of the crossing and that the remaining four bays, behind the altar, formed a separate chapel. This is likely to have housed the shrine of St Ninian. The arrangement implies an aisled presbytery in order to provide easy access to the shrine.

The southern chapel was designed for two altars, one standing in each bay of the long eastern wall. This chapel was probably added to provide a more spacious setting for the shrine. No ancient masonry is now visible at this upper level.

Access to the vaults beneath (see photograph on page 11) is by means of a door in the end wall of the southern chapel. The space under this chapel is covered with a wide barrel-vault, most of which is medieval in date, and is lighted by two windows, one in each bay of the east wall. From here one passes through a fifteenth-century doorway, cut in the older wall, into the crypt beneath the eastern chapel. The original access to this crypt was from the church by stairs in the thickness of the north wall. These stairs have been blocked but the lower treads are still visible just west of the outer door. The crypt is covered by two barrel-vaults running north-south and resting on a central wall. These are insertions of about 1500. Originally there was a groined vault springing from the corbels in the angles and in the centres of the side walls and resting on a central pier. The corbels and springers of this vault can be seen in the north-west and north-east corners and in the centre of the north side, where the masonry has been cut back to expose the earlier work. The carefully finished freestone dressings date from about 1200 and mark the first stage in the building of the Premonstratensian priory church.

From the north door of the crypt one passes across a small court into a restored fourteenth-century building. This is now approximately square but the foundations outside show that it originally extended further east. The purpose of the building is uncertain. It does not appear to have been vaulted, with its main floor level with the church, but the modern work may have disguised the evidence. If it were really on two levels the building might be explained as a sacristy. It is, however, possible that it only existed at the lower level and thus formed a part of the conventual arrangement.

The Early Christian Church

The area immediately outside the east end of the church was cleared by the Marquess of Bute and the ancient remains marked out by modern dwarf walls at the slightly higher new ground level. No old stone-work is now visible.

Projecting eastward from the wall of the crypt is a rectangular building 4·6 m wide over walls 1 m thick. As marked out, the north wall is thickened by a wedge of masonry ending in a small buttress beyond the face of the east wall. Excavation has shown that this arrangement was not part of the original structure and that its foundation lay at a higher level. It may have formed part of the wall of the medieval cemetery.

The walls of the original structure were constructed of roughly split, undressed blocks of local stone set in clay. Outside the masonry had been daubed with a cream-colour plaster, portions of which were found still adhering to the base of the wall face. The west end of the building was cut away by the end wall of the crypt and it is now impossible to establish its full size.

The area in which this building stands lay near the heart of the Celtic monastery. A number of early Christian stones, including the oldest inscription (No 1, p. 27), were found close by. The discovery of a light-coloured plaster on the face of the masonry inevitably recalls Bede's description of *Candida Casa* (White House), so called from its church of stone. Dry-built structures of stone were not unknown in the district and a church of this type would hardly have earned the fame which Bede's words suggest. It was the white covering which distinguished the original church of St Ninian and the discovery near the centre of the monastery of a primitive building treated in this manner perhaps justifies the conclusion that this was indeed the 'White House'.

(See pp. 25–32 for the Catalogue of Stones)

St Ninian's Chapel was probably built for the convenience of pilgrims arriving by sea, and may have been erected about 1300 as a replacement for an earlier chapel. This drawing, by General Pitt-Rivers, is dated 1887.

St Ninian's Chapel, Isle of Whithorn

The Isle of Whithorn lies on the east coast of the Machars 5 km south-east of Whithorn. The island, which is now joined to the mainland by a causeway, consists of two rounded hills linked by an isthmus. On the west between the island and the coast is a sheltered inlet largely dry at low water; this must always have been the principal harbour for sea-traffic to Whithorn. In the medieval period it would have been the port of entry for pilgrims coming from Ireland and the Isle of Man as well as those who preferred a coasting vessel to the hazards of land travel.

On the seaward slope of the inner hill are the ruins of a small chapel standing in a walled enclosure. The rectangular building, measuring 9·5 m by 5 m, was partly rebuilt in 1898 by the Marquess of Bute. The door is on the south side, near the west end. There is a two-light window with chamfered dressings of hard local stone in the east wall and small lancets with widely splayed embrasures and similar dressings in each of the side walls. Traces of a bench were found extending along most of the west end and the west part of the north wall.

The building may have been erected about 1300 as a replacement for an earlier chapel. Excavations revealed the foundations of an older chancel rather narrower than the present building, with a chancel arch some 5 m from the west end. Though difficult to date, a building of this type would not be older than the twelfth century. Traces of a stone enclosure wall are visible around the chapel.

The chapel was probably built for the convenience of pilgrims arriving by sea. There was no trace of early Christian remains and no crosses or memorials of this period are recorded from the Isle of Whithorn.

St Ninian's Cave, Glasserton

St Ninian's Cave, on the south coast of the Machars, about 400 m west of the mouth of Physgill Glen and some 5 km south of Whithorn, has long been associated with St Ninian. Following the discovery of an incised cross here in 1871, further crosses were subsequently detected and excavations were carried out in 1884. The cave was then cleared down to a stone pavement. A number of crosses cut on boulders and loose fragments of stone were found. They have now been removed to the museum at Whithorn for safe-keeping (p. 30; see also photograph on page 6).

Though the excavations showed that the stone pavement and occupation debris were largely of comparatively recent origin, the discovery of crosses, cut both on the rock faces and on stones proves that the cave was frequented by pilgrims to the shrine of St Ninian. Some of these crosses go back at least as far as the eighth century and there is no reason to doubt the connection of the cave with St Ninian himself.

Seven crosses of early form are cut into the rock on the west side of the cave. The first lies some 6 m outside the mouth of the cave—a small simple cross with T-shaped ends to the arms. There is a group of four crosses 2 m from the cave mouth. The uppermost has been recut and is incised in outline with expanded arms and a small dot marking the centre of the head. Below this are three other crosses of similar form, cut in a row about 300 mm apart. The outermost is finished with a pointed base, that in the centre is equal-armed with two lines forming a long shaft continuing down the rock face, and the third is so weathered as to be virtually indistinguishable. Two further crosses, similar to the last described, can be seen within the cave, the first 5 m from the inner end of the cave, the second 2 m further in.

All the crosses are executed in the pocked technique used on early Christian memorial stones. They can only have been votives, cut by pilgrims as a record of their visit, a permanent memorial of offerings made in honour of St Ninian. They are of a form found in the eighth and ninth centuries but the type may have survived later. The outermost cross should be even earlier, a relic of the Celtic church before the Northumbrian conquest of Galloway.

Some of the stones and crosses in St Ninian's Cave, shortly before their removal to the museum at Whithorn.

Chapel Finian, Mochrum

Chapel Finian lies on the west coast of the Machars, in the parish of Mochrum, 19 km north-west of Whithorn. Excavation in 1950 uncovered the remains of a rectangular building measuring 6·7 m from east to west and 4·1 m transversely within walls 700 mm thick. The walls were of large blocks of stone split and roughly dressed on their outer face and bonded with mortar. Each of the two side walls had three external buttresses, one in the centre and one against each corner. There was one entrance, through the south wall midway between the central and southern buttresses. It had no door checks, for the hollows on the inner angles formerly held large upright stones—one of which survives close by where it fell. There was no trace of any windows, the walls being altogether too ruinous. There were, however, signs of a stone bench, perhaps encased in wood, running along the eastern part of the south wall. The building is enclosed within a sub-rectangular dry-stone boundary with a stone-lined well immediately outwith it on the south-west.

St Finian, founder of a monastery at Moville, County Down, who died about 588, is traditionally associated with Whithorn. The plan of the chapel, however, suggests that it dates from a time subsequent to St Finian's ministry and it is likely that the chapel was erected in the tenth or eleventh century for the use of pilgrims coming from Ireland to St Ninian's shrine at Whithorn.

Laggangairn Standing Stones, New Luce

Two large, upright stones, each bearing a carving of a cross, stand close to each other in bleak moorland 15 km north of Glenluce. They are said to have formed part of a circle of fourteen stones, presumably dating from the Bronze Age (2000–700 BC), the missing stones having been removed over the centuries, some as lintels for neighbouring farm-steadings. The crosses, identical and assuming the form of an expanded-arm Latin cross no more than a metre high with incised crosslets in each of the four angles, are dated to between the seventh and ninth centuries on stylistic grounds and may conceivably have marked a stopping-place for pilgrims on their way to the shrine of St Ninian at Whithorn from Carrick and the west of Scotland.

Laggangairn Standing Stones, drawn by General Pitt-Rivers, the first Inspector of Ancient Monuments, who was responsible for the transfer of the stones into State care in 1887.

A general view of Chapel Finian.

This cross (No. 7) dating to the tenth century, is typical of the Whithorn School. It served as the headstone of a grave.

CATALOGUE OF STONES

The Early Christian Monuments

The earliest Christian monuments in the Celtic lands are the memorial stones found in Wales, south-west England and the Lowlands of Scotland. These stones were erected to commemorate priests and chieftains and originally stood above their graves. Many are inscribed simply with the name of the deceased. Sometimes this is preceded by a simple formula, such as *Hic jacet* (here lies). A few bear Christian symbols of various types. The chronology of these memorials is established by the fact that their phraseology and lettering follow Continental practice and can, to a certain extent, be dated. In Wales and Cornwall a few personal names have been identified and dated in other sources.

The greatest concentration of such stones in the north is in Galloway. Three, from Whithorn and Kirkmadrine, are now on display, together with two other allied inscriptions. They would originally have stood in the Christian cemeteries that encircled the ancient churches.

In addition to their inscriptions, all save the earliest of the stones found in Galloway bear unmistakable Christian symbols. All four are carved with the Chi-rho, which reproduced the first two letters of the name of Christ, written in the Greek form (ΧΡΙΣΤΟΣ). This is a usage common on the Continent; the form found in Scotland is the later of the two known types. One of the stones at Kirkmadrine (K.1) bears in addition another Christian symbol, the Alpha and Omega, which is found on a number of other early Christian memorials. A second (K.3) uses a variant, the words *initium et finis* (the Beginning and the End). Both are emblematic of Christ, in allusion to Revelations XXI, 6.

A further instance of the imitation of Continental usage occurs on the oldest stone from Whithorn (No. 1) on which the surviving relative, in this case the grandson, records his erection of the monument.

None of these stones found can be dated by external evidence but the series would seem to range from the fifth to the seventh century.

The Whithorn School of Crosses

Whithorn was at the heart of the area of Norse settlement in Galloway and here, beside the old shrine of St Ninian, was the burial place of the new ruling class. Parts of some twenty standing crosses have been found, small headstones designed to mark individual graves. The typical cross of this Whithorn school (No. 7 is the only complete example) is a flat slab of stone with a circular head and splayed shaft. On the head is carved in low relief a cross with expanded arms separated by circular sinkings; a small boss generally marks the centre of the head and others may occur in the four sinkings, or these may be pierced through. Interlace generally covers the shaft and sometimes extends into the head. As far as is known all these crosses came from the old graveyard at Whithorn and some were found near the early church. Crosses of similar type are known from a number of old church sites in the Machars.

Only two of the crosses—one from Whithorn (No. 10), one from St Ninian's Cave (C.4)—are inscribed. In both cases the inscription is incomplete but the formulae are of types found in other areas of Norse

The Monreith Cross (No. 40), the finest of the Whithorn school of crosses, now on display in the museum.

settlement. The inscriptions are in Anglian runes and the ornament on the crosses is of a type datable to the late tenth or eleventh century. Similar crosses are known in a number of areas occupied by the Scandinavians who adapted the old Anglian tradition of memorial to their own taste.

The cross with a disc head, the characteristic mark of the Whithorn school, represents a coalescence of two ideas. The old engraved pillar with a cross set in a circle had long been established in Galloway and elsewhere. At Whithorn there are no examples later than the stone inscribed with the name of St Peter but in the Isle of Man there is a slab with the name of Gwriad, a ruler of the early ninth century. This traditional type of memorial was influenced by the free-standing cross elaborated in Northumbria and Ireland. The resulting memorial retained the traditional form of the engraved cross set in a circle but the background was cut away and the resulting surface enriched with ornamental designs drawn from Northumbrian art as modified by Norse taste.

The Whithorn school includes not only headstones marking individual graves but also a number of large crosses. The finest of these, the Monreith Cross (No. 40), stands over 2 m high. The shaft of another from Kirkland of Longcastle (No. 21), an ancient church site north-west of Whithorn, is also in the museum. These tall shafts represent what a West Saxon writer termed: 'the standard of the holy cross erected on the estates of nobles and lifted up on high so as to be convenient for the frequency of daily prayer'. They were often set up to mark cemeteries or sites set apart for religious purposes at a time when churches were rare outwith the monasteries and services might be held in the open. Fragments of crosses of this type have been found at a number of church sites in the Machars, including Penninghame, Wigtown and Longcastle. These sites are not necessarily new foundations of the Norse period; the crosses may well represent only new and finer symbols on ancient sites which go back to the earliest Christian days.

The inscribed crosses (C.1 and 2) show that St Ninian's Cave continued to be used in this period. The other crosses found in the cave, both those cut on the rock face and those roughly carved on loose stones, are difficult to date. Some at least seem to go back to the period of Northumbrian rule but one group is influenced by the monuments of the Whithorn school; these stones, on which are cut circles containing four symmetrically disposed circles each with a central dot, clearly imitate the most distinctive features of the normal headstone.

The collection from Kirkmadrine also includes monuments of this period (K.5 and 6). These are all small and suggest that the site was no longer of much importance.

The Whithorn Stones

1. Roughly squared pillar stone with inscription, found in 1891, probably near the early church. The inscription in twelve horizontal lines reads:

TE DOMINU(M)/ LAUDAMUS/ LATINUS/ ANNORU(M)/ XXXV ET/ FILIA SUA/ ANN(ORUM) IV/ (H)IC SI(G)NUM/ FECERUT/ NEPUS/ BARROVA/ DI

"We praise thee Lord. Latinus, aged thirty-five, and his daughter, aged four. The grandson Barrovadus set up the monument here"

The letters, though some are carelessly formed, are all Roman capitals. The allusion in the opening words is to the 146th psalm (*I will praise the Lord in my life*), which forms part of the Roman office for the dead. The erection of the memorial stone by the surviving relative is frequently attested in early Christian memorials. The pillar was a gravestone and dates from the middle of the fifth century. It is the earliest Christian memorial in Scotland.

2. Squared stone pillar with cross and inscription, which formerly stood by the side of the road south of Whithorn (see photograph on page 5). On the front is incised a cross with curved expanded arms set within a double circle; the cross is formed of four segments of circles which intersect near the centre of the enclosing circle. The right hand line of the top arm of the cross serves as the upright of a capital R. The cross and circle are set on a short stem with a flat base and curved sides. On the stem is cut a capital T; to the right is a short curved line, possibly the bungled setting out of the stem. To

The Latinus Stone (No. 1).

the left of the stem and continuing below it across the full width of the stone is cut in three lines:

[L]OCI/ PETRI APU/ STOLI
"The place of Peter the Apostle"

The letters are straggling and uneven, with forked serifs and the uprights of the P and R rising above the top of the loops. This type of letter belongs to Merovingian Gaul, where it went out of fashion during the eighth century; it is very rare in the British Isles.

A *locus* is a place, possibly a cemetery, with perhaps a small oratory, dedicated to God in honour of a saint. The phrase and the use of the Gaulish alphabet suggest Celtic rather than Saxon connections, and a date in the seventh century is indicated.

3. Lower part of a cross shaft, found in the churchyard at Whithorn. The front and back of the shaft are each filled with a single panel of well designed, regular interlace. This fragment, still in the pure Anglian tradition, is a late example dating from the late eighth–early ninth century.

4. Head of a cross. On the front is a cross with expanded arms set in a sunk circle. On the back is an incised spiral within a circle. The purpose of the monument is uncertain but the rough form is an early feature and the well drawn cross may be of the eighth or ninth century.

5. Part of a rectangular cross shaft, broken at both ends, which formerly stood at the manse and presumably came from the churchyard. On the front are two panels, the upper with a well-designed interlace, the lower with two standing figures. These are draped, with crescentric headdresses or halos, and each appears to be holding something in the right hand. They probably represent saints. On the back and sides are panels of poorly designed interlace; the lower panel on the back has rough diagonal scored lines in place of the interlace.

The shaft belonged to a more elaborate cross which was probably erected within the precincts of the monastery to commemorate some event. The decoration is a late example of the type produced by the Northumbrians and probably dates from the tenth century.

6. Small slab, found in the cemetery at Whithorn. Two small crosses flank a larger central cross. This has expanded ends to the head and arms and rectangular panels imitated from the jewelled ornament which adorned the more elaborate early crosses. The design represents the Crucified Christ between the two thieves and follows the ancient tradition which did not show the figure of Christ on the cross. The slab is probably architectural and the form of the crosses and ornament suggest a date in the ninth century.

The remainder are monuments of the Whithorn school, many found in or near the churchyards in which they were originally erected. The earliest are Nos. 7, 8 and 9, which date from the tenth century. None of the others can have been made much before the year 1000 and many must belong to the eleventh century.

7. Headstone (see photograph on page 24). The circular head has a small central boss and expanded arms, the terminals of which are separated by shallow grooves; there are circular sinkings between the arms. The plain cross has a slight beaded outline. The shaft is filled with a single panel of firmly designed interlace. The roughly dressed back is plain.

8. Headstone. On both sides of the circular head is a plain cross with expanded arms, the ends separated by a slight groove; bosses mark the centre of the head and the circular spaces between the arms. On each face of the shaft is a panel of interlace, the strands emphasised by a slight central groove. One of the interlaced designs includes rings.

9. Part of cross shaft, the front decorated with an interlace; on one edge is a row of interlinked rings.

10. Headstone, found built into a house in Whithorn. On the front is a plain cross with a small central boss and expanded arms; the shaft is filled with crudely designed interlace with pellets among the strands, which have a central groove. This type of interlace is common in Norse-period carvings in south-west Cumbria. On the back is a similar cross, also with interlace and pellets on the shaft. The top and one edge have a continuous T pattern. On the other edge is a mutilated inscription in Anglian runes, which may read:

[BECUN DON]FERTHS
"The monument (or cross) of Donferth"

11. Lower end of cross shaft. On the front is a panel of interlace with four vertical rows of rings. On the back are two knots separated by a cable moulding. The strands of both faces are emphasised by a central groove.

12. Lower end of cross shaft. On the front is a panel of interlace with three vertical rows of rings. On the back a similar design is engraved in outline; the background has not been cut away, leaving the design unfinished. On both faces the strands are marked with central grooves.

13. On the front is the base of a circular head, on which was a cross with expanded arms, similar to No. 7 but with the sinkings separating the arms completely pierced. The shaft is filled with a panel of irregular interlace, the strands of which are marked by central grooves. Near the centre a shield-shaped sinking has been cut away leaving two chevrons in relief and the letters A M, the arms and initials of the man for whom the stone was reused in the eighteenth century. The back of the head is similar to the front and the shaft has a panel of widely spaced interlace.

14. On the front is a cross with a slight central boss and expanded arms, separated by circles. A wide pelleted border encloses the cross. The shaft has a panel of irregular interlace, the strands marked by a central groove. On the back a similar cross within a plain border fills the head. Cross and shaft are filled with a continuous interlace of the same type as that on the front.

15. Fragment of a cross head, of the normal type with a central boss and four sinkings between the arms. On each arm is a knot and the back is plain.

16–19. Fragments of cross shafts, each with panels of interlace and other ornament of normal type.

20. Rectangular cross slab, found on the farm of Craiglemine, 3 km north-west of Whithorn. On the face is an irregular cross with expanded arms, standing on a long shaft. The cross is formed by cutting away the background, which is pocked. The two sides are dressed along natural lines of cleavage; the back is left rough. The slab probably formed part of the cover of a tomb and is not earlier than the twelfth century.

21. Cross Shaft. The head of the cross is broken; at the foot is a tenon, by which the cross was secured in a stone base. It was found built into a barn at Kirkland of Longcastle, an ancient church site. The base of the circular head shows that it was plain with a beaded outline to the cross. The arms were separated by circular holes, as in No. 13 and the complete example in Kirkinner church. The shaft is crowded with a panel of loosely designed interlace, each strand being marked with a central groove. A single pellet occurs near the lower right corner. The ornament on the reverse is similar, with the interlace less coherently drawn. The tall shaft suggests that the monument was designed as a cemetery cross, perhaps late in the tenth century.

22. Headstone, found built into a byre at Boghouse farm, adjacent to the church in Mochrum. On the front a cross with a long shaft and slightly expanded arms is formed by cutting away the background of a panel with an arched head and tapered sides; the cross is thrown into relief by pocking the background; it stands on an irregular panel filled with incised diagonal lines. On the back a cross is indicated by four sunk circles marking the spaces between the arms. At the centre of the head is a small boss. On one edge is a small panel of badly designed two-strand interlace. The other edge is plain.

23. Headstone, found at Boghouse farm with No. 22. On the front are two crosses incised in outline with deeply cut lines of V-section. The upper cross has a wedge-shaped head and arms and a long, slightly swollen shaft. The lower cross has four unequal wedge-shaped arms, the shaft noticeably smaller than the head. On the back is a cross similar to the first described, but with a plain shaft; it is obliquely set.

24. Part of a slab, found at Elrig, in the parish of Mochrum. The only ornamented face has a cross with expanded arms, filled with a continuous interlaced pattern. On the shaft of the cross is a panel of frets framed with a cable moulding.

A part of a head of the normal Whithorn type was found during the building of the modern house at Elrig and is now built into the front wall. A third slab, a portion of a shaft with interlace, is built into the barn at Airylick, a short distance away. All these are of the tenth or eleventh century and suggest that the land was then connected with some ecclesiastical establishment.

25. Fragment with incised cross-head and evidence of loop-work below, from Brighouse farm, near Whithorn.

26–35. Fragments of crosses of normal type found at Whithorn (with the exception of No. 34, from Gleniron Several, Old Luce).

36. Cross slab, found at Whithorn. On the front a cross, carved in relief and with expanded arms. The shaft is incised and bears an

inscription in Anglian runes, now illegible as the memorial was later used as a paving-stone. It is probably of seventh- or eighth-century date.

37. Shaft of a headstone, similar to No. 7, found reused as a building-stone at the north-east corner of the priory nave.

38. Shaft of an upright cross, with interlace pattern bordered by cablework on both faces, found at Whithorn.

39. Tapered grave-stone, with an incised Latin type cross with a second cross-head above it, found at Whithorn.

40. The Monreith Cross—a well-preserved and almost perfect example of a disc-headed standing cross of the Whithorn school, dated to the tenth century (see photograph on page 26). It is said to have stood near the Old Place of Monreith, the original home of the Maxwells of Monreith, prior to its removal in the mid-nineteenth century to Monreith House. The late Sir Aylmer Maxwell agreed to its transfer, in 1973, to the museum for safe-keeping.

Stones from St Ninian's Cave

In addition to the votive crosses cut on the rock, St Ninian's Cave has produced a number of crosses on loose pieces of stone (see photograph on page 22). Many of these are very rough, and the greater number are probably votive, though one (C.4) is clearly a headstone.

C.1. Boulder with an incised cross with flattened, slightly forked ends. This rough votive is not closely datable but the form of the cross may be as old as the seventh century.

C.2. Two fragments of a broken stone slab. In the centre is a carefully cut double circle within which are four smaller circles, each containing an equal armed cross with forked ends. Part of a similar cross appears near one corner of the slab, the other corners are damaged or missing. The form of the crosses indicates a date in the eighth century and the size and design of the slab suggest the cover of the hollow containing the relics in an altar.

C.3. Wedge-shaped pillar, possibly a headstone. On the face is cut an equal armed cross in a circle; below is a smaller cross of the same type with a long shaft reaching to the base of the stone. The design is in the late Northumbrian tradition and probably belongs to the ninth century.

C.4. Headstone, reused as a paving slab. On the front is a cross with expanded arms separated by circles. Both cross and shaft are covered with interlace; the pattern is badly set out and the strands have a central groove. At the base was an inscription in two or more lines of Anglian runes. Only the word [WR]OTE (made) remains at the end of the first line. This is part of a common formula, which runs 'X made this cross for Y; pray for his soul'.

The headstone dates from the eleventh century and must originally have stood in or near the cave. A skeleton was found in the outer part of the cave in 1884. It is possible that the interment was that of a hermit, possibly a member of the community of Whithorn, who had retired to the cave, and that the cross was set up to mark his grave.

C.5. A tall pillar stone. On the top of one face is cut an equal-armed cross in a circle, with a small cross marking the centre. Below are two crosses in circles, the arms marked by four smaller circles. This design, which is also found on some of the votive crosses, links this group with the crosses of the Whithorn school of the tenth and eleventh centuries.

C.6.–C.11. Votive crosses on rough slabs of stone, the first three influenced by the Whithorn school and so datable to the late tenth or eleventh century.

C.12. Roughly squared slab of shale found set into the pavement uncovered in 1884. Letters scratched on the surface may read:

SANCT(TO) NINIA(NO)

The letters are comparatively modern and the votive offering may have been from some Catholic fugitive who visited the cave during the penal times of the late sixteenth or seventeenth century.

C.13.–C.18. Miscellaneous stones.

The Kirkmadrine Stones

This ancient church site lies in the parish of Stoneykirk in the Rhinns of Galloway. Three early inscribed stones and a number of pre-Romanesque cross fragments have been found at various times which show that the site was of some importance, probably a monastery, in the early Christian period. In the medieval period the site was used for a parish church.

K.1. Roughly squared pillar stone with cross and inscription on the front. Found within the old burial ground. On the front, at the top, is cut a cross with slightly expanded arms, set within a circle. There is a loop on the right side of the upper arm, so that the whole forms the Christian monogram, known as the Chi-rho. Above the circle are the letters A et (O) and, below, a Latin inscription in six horizontal lines:

HIC IACENT/ S(AN)C(T)I ET PRAE/ CIPUI SACER/ DOTES IDES/ VIVENTIUS/ ET MAVORIUS
"Here lie the holy and chief priests, Ides, Viventius and Mavorius".

The term 'chief priests' should probably be interpreted as 'Bishops', implying that Kirkmadrine was one of the principal evangelistic centres in this part of Scotland. The letters are good, well cut, Roman capitals with a number of ligatures. The pillar was a memorial, set up to mark the burial place of the priests, and dates from the fifth century.

K.2. Pillar similar to K.1 above. The cross and monogram are similar, but the Alpha and Omega do not appear. The Latin inscription in three horizontal lines reads:

......S ET/ FLOREN/ TIUS
"(Here lie)......s and Florentius".

Various attempts have been made to decipher the first name but with no success. The memorial was set up in the late fifth century.

K.3. Roughly squared pillar, similar to the above. The cross has thicker and heavier arms with pronounced wedge-shaped ends and below is a Latin inscription in two horizontal lines:

INITIUM/ ET FINIS
"The beginning and the end"

The allusion is to a passage from Revelations, used to indicate that the stone was a cross of Christ, probably set up to indicate a space used for worship. The more advanced character of the cross and lettering indicate a date around 600.

A number of fragmentary monuments of a later date have been found at various times in the churchyard, indicating that the site continued to be used for burials. The style of these varies in several respects from the monuments of the Whithorn school but they cover the same period. The more important of these are listed below; the first three are headstones, the use of the other two is uncertain but they were probably funerary.

K.4. At the top is a cross with a large square centre and angular T-shaped head and arms; the short shaft rises from a large square base divided into four by diagonal lines, each compartment containing a small incised cross. The design is in

This monument (K.1) to the three priests, Ides, Viventius and Mavorius, was found at the ancient ecclesiastical site of Kirkmadrine.

the Anglian tradition and similar crosses are known in the eighth and ninth centuries.

K.5. On one face is a Maltese cross with a slight central boss. Curved horn-like objects spring from the angles between the arms. Below are two crosses each with a central boss and expanded arms. The design is in the late Northumbrian tradition and probably dates from the ninth or early tenth century.

K.6. At the top is a cross with expanded arms separated by circles. The surface of the cross is filled with linear ornament. Below is a plain cross with a small central boss. Below again is an ornamental lozenge. The stone is wedge-shaped, a late feature (cf. No. 22), and the ornament indicates a date in the eleventh century.

K.7. At the top of the small pillar is a cross with straight arms and square angles; there is a slight boss in the centre. In each corner below the arms are three curved lines springing from the horizontal base on which the cross stands and joining the shaft. The form of cross suggests a twelfth-century date.

K.8. At the top is a panel of irregular and debased interlace. A second panel has a cross with T-shaped ends to the head and arms and a leaf-shaped expansion at the foot of the shaft. The slab is not earlier than the twelfth century.

Further Reading

J Romilly Allen, *The Early Christian Monuments of Scotland,* (Edinburgh, 1903)

Royal Commission on the Ancient and Historical Monuments of Scotland, *County of Wigtown,* (London, 1912)

W G Collingwood, *Northumbrian Crosses of the Pre-Norman Age,* (1927)

W D Simpson, *St Ninian and the Origins of the Christian Church in Scotland,* (Edinburgh, 1940)

C A R Radford, 'Excavations at Whithorn 1949', *Trans. Dumfriesshire Galloway Nat. Hist. Antiq. Soc.,* XXVII, (1948-49), 85-126

C A R Radford, 'The excavations at Chapel Finian, Mochrum', *Trans. Dumfriesshire Galloway Nat. Hist. Antiq. Soc.,* XXVIII, (1949-50), 28-40

C A R Radford, 'St Ninian's Cave', *Trans. Dumfriesshire Galloway Nat. Hist. Antiq. Soc.,* XXVIII, (1950-51), 96-98

C A R Radford and G Donaldson, 'Post Reformation Church at Whithorn', *Proc. Soc. Antiq. Scot., 85,* (1950-51), 117-33

C A R Radford, 'Excavations at Whithorn (Final Report)', *Trans. Dumfriesshire Galloway Nat. Hist. Antiq. Soc.,* XXXIV, (1955-56), 131-94

C Thomas, *The Early Christian Archaeology of North Britain,* (Oxford, 1971)

R N Bailey, *Viking Sculpture in Northern England,* (1980)

R Fawcett, *Scottish Medieval Churches,* (Edinburgh, 1985)

Printed in Scotland by McCorquodale (Scotland) Ltd.
Dd 287289/4429 C40 3/89